Until we meet again

A collection of poems

Betty Olga Jump

1917-2012

Spinnaker Press

Portsmouth and Gosport
Hampshire, England
2015

Published in 2015
by Spinnaker Press

© Lynette Lord, 2015

ISBN: 978-0-95666 19-5-1

Cover images: *front cover,* Betty Jump (1941),
Back cover, anticlockwise from top right: Betty Jump with
Gabrielle, 1942
Portsmouth Guildhall bombed, *The News,* Portsmouth
Blenheim above Portsmouth, photo Lynette Lord
Betty Jump at a fancy dress ball, 1938
Betty Jump dancing, 1924
Princes Theatre, Portsmouth, after bombing, photo *The News,*
Portsmouth
Southsea Pier, acrylic painting by Lynette Lord
(all photos of Betty owned by her family)

Spinnaker Press thanks *The News* for kind permission to
reproduce the photographs of the Guildhall and Princes
Theatre

Cover design by Jackie Plummer, i-i design.com, Portsmouth

Spinnaker Press, 21 Solent Way, Gosport PO12 2NR England

Printed by Biddles Books Limited, Kings Lynn, UK

Contents

Betty Olga Jump - a short biography   v
by Lynette Lord

When I return from war   1
A farewell   2
A longing   3
My wish for you   4
To my brother   5
Window of dreams   6
Odd thoughts   7
Unspoken Love   8
I wish that I may see   9
My love for you   10
My love is like the south-west wind   11
Thoughts of you   12
Force of Nature   13
The Arab cloak   14
Yet life goes by   15
New chapters   16
Winter evenings   18
Lost paradise   19
Heart's loneliness   20
A requiem   21
War dreams   22
A German woman's lament   23
The promised land   24
Voices from the sea   26

The secret of the sea   27
Depression   28
After the nightmare   29
Boy? Man!   30
Intellectual heights   31
To my mother   32
Peace   33

Poems written after 1946

Was and Is   36
The lost child   37
Lament for a dead child   38
Shades and echoes   39
The lost love   40
Pussy willow   41
Joe the dog   42
The wedding   43
When I was young and sad   44
What is poetry?   45
A practical man   46
The re-arranged   47
Time's twist   48
Years passed   49
The lake   50
The last spring   51
My son   52
The real world   53
Ode to pain   54
My blessing   55
All my loves   56

Betty Olga Jump

a brief biography

Betty Jump belongs to a group of war poets which remains very little known – the 'war wives' of World War II. Like others, her short lyrical poems were not written for publication, but to define for herself her strong, and often painful, feelings. These poems – tender, unsophisticated, direct and always sincere – capture the mood of a generation of women who suffered through the war while not involved in military action.

She experienced the bombing at first hand, worked from the centre of Portsmouth on the child-evacuee programme while living locally. A direct hit on their air raid shelter killed seven members of her family, and she lived in daily fear for her husband Kenneth, a sailor involved in most of the major sea battles, and for her brother, who fought in Burma for four years. For all that, she relished the joys of motherhood and also the brief and often frantic social life when the troops came to Portsmouth.

A family visit to Porchester Castle, Portsmouth Harbour (1958).
Back row: Kenneth, Betty, Lynette and Gabrielle;
front row: Steve and Betty's niece Sally

Betty Jump wrote poetry throughout her life, and many of these poems were found among her effects following her death in 2012. She was widely read and largely self-educated, having been compelled to leave school at 13 – although she had just won second prize in a regional story-writing competition.

She was already familiar with family hardship. Her father, initially a wealthy businessman and later farmer, developed post-traumatic stress disorder after World War I service transporting ammunition to the Front Line. His business and then his farm failed. Betty, then a young child, remembered the bailiffs carrying off their possessions, and the family moving into a rented basement in Landport, then a decayed area of Portsmouth.

Betty's father broke down, and never worked again. It was left to Betty's mother to provide an income for the family by renting and running a guesthouse in Albert Grove, which narrowly escaped being demolished by a WW2 bomb.

In autumn 1946 Betty's husband Kenneth was demobbed, and returned to his previous job in Manchester, whilst he was searching for a suitable home for the family. In November, Betty's mother suddenly and unexpectedly died, aged 50. Betty immediately left her job in the city treasurer's office and took over her mother's guest house, as they had to give the residents three months notice to leave. Betty and Gabrielle (aged 4) travelled to the north in mid March 1947, after the terrible winter snow and floods delayed them by 2 weeks, leaving behind Betty's beloved Portsmouth for over 40 years. Betty and Kenneth had three more children, but lost the youngest, Louise, at 5 months.

Despite these tragedies, Betty committed herself to voluntary work, initially supporting the parents of terminally ill children, then working in a Red Cross scheme at a psychiatric hospital. For many years, she also helped at a local play school.

Betty and Ken finally returned to south Hampshire in the 1990s. They lived in Waterlooville until Ken died in 2008. Betty stayed on until 2010, when she moved to Croft Manor Care Home in Fareham. She died there, in her 96th year, in December 2012.

Lynette Lord , 2015

Spinnaker Press and Lynette Lord acknowledge
with thanks the assistance of the Portsmouth-based
poets who read and advised on the selection of
poems for this book.

Maggie Sawkins
George Marsh
M. L. McCarthy
Denise Bennett

When I Return From War

A garden sweet with the song of birds
A book with wise and kindly words
A dawning day with soft blue haze
Peaceful nights and warm bright days
Oh Lord please keep these things in store
For me when I return from War.

Deep in the country, lazy hours
Warm golden corn, and poppy flowers
A flowing stream with darting fish
Oh Lord please grant this simple wish.

Above all let my loved one be
Waiting my coming, tenderly.
Let all troubled years between
Help make our future more serene.

(1940s)

A Farewell

When you are gone, my Darling, I shall go
Down to the sea – to stand a while below
Those cloudy skies that held such friendly stars,
Those nights and mornings when there was no time –
No world beyond our space, no clocks to chime,
 – Togetherness 'neath soft blue sky – and stars.

(1945)

A Longing

All through the still of night
My heart cries out to you
Through endless hours, till light
In little ribbons, through
The curtains creeps.

All through the dragging day
My soul seeks only you
In each small thought I pray
The hours will hurry through
Until you come.

And when you come at last
Love sings deep within me
When happiness is past
I'll have this memory
Within my heart.

(1940s)

My Wish For You

I wish that your eyes may behold the grace of trees
The Paleness of the moon, and the surge of stormy seas.
That you may hear sweetness in the song of birds
The heaven in Music and the beauty of words.
That your mind may, with ease, discern gold from dross
And your spirit have faith to surmount grief or loss.
That your lips only utter the nicest of things.
Kindness and gentleness. A happy heart that sings.
These all are life's treasures, such things I cannot give
But I wish you may have them as long as you live.

(1944)

To My Brother

A photograph arrived today
He had been 18 months away
In Burma fighting fiendish Japs.
And there's the difference perhaps.

His photo just before he went
Shows boyish face – no great portent
Of sternness that's embodied now
In steely eyes and low'ring brow.

A boy left – a man will return
And Mother! though your heart will yearn
You cannot help but proudly say

My Son?! He is a Man today.

(1940s)

Window of Dreams

I know a window with a view
Of tree tops, spires and sky.
Of wispy clouds across the moon
Above a city high.

There's breathing space to be alone
In quiet solitude
To sit a while and gaze upon
A sunset's magnitude.

The after dusk of hazy blue
A slim young rising moon
And dawn in shades of grey and rose,
Cathedral bells sweet tune
Calling before the busy day
Begins with frantic rush

Reminding us of holy peace
And spiritual hush.

(1940s)

Odd Thoughts

Moonlight on a frozen lake
Sweet golden gorse at sunset
Bird's soft song to bid 'awake'
Spring leaves all gently rain wet.

The drone-y hum of summer bees.
The surge and sweep of stormy seas
The gallant sight of billowed sails
Exhilaration of swift gales.

(1940s)

Unspoken Love

Tonight I heard a robin sing
His song was not of earth or spring.
Not yet the infant breeze – nor skies
His song was of my Lover's eyes.

He trilled the warmth and tenderness
Gave voice to my heart's shy caress
Which never have I strength to give
To him for whom, alone, I live.

(1940s)

I Wish That You May See

I wish that you may see – not just a tree
But a leafy pictured rhapsody,
A Summer fantasy of light
And shade, and rustles in the night.

How can I tell my love for you?
I've tried, it seems, my whole life thro'
For words to say so tenderly.

(1940s)

My Love for You

You ask what is my love for you?
– The deepest depth of Midnight Blue
The sweetest notes in any tune

More golden than the Harvest Moon.
A sweeter scented flower ne'er grew
More fragrant than my love for you.

(1940s)

My Love is Like the South West Wind

My Love is like the South West wind
Strong and fierce and swift
I hear him calling me and find
His perfect gift
Of Love my Soul and body needs.
My weakling feet
Fair would follow where 'ere he speeds
But he's too fleet.

So I've to be content with him,
To send my heart -
No! – that's just a foolish whim –
Of him I'm part
And though he leaves me here at times
To journey fast
I go with him to Foreign Climes
Both first and last.

(1940s)

11

Shadowed Things

My thoughts of you cannot be shadowed things
To put away as part of Life's drear order
But swiftly they take flight, with shining wings
To battle with that dread Marauder
Depression, who o'er sweeps my darkened mind
And with insidious passion tries to kill
Each little thought of loveliness I find.

Without my thoughts of you I'd have no will
To face the weary years that lie ahead
When you are gone and I go on alone
And all the tears from my poor heart have bled
And turned into a dear 'Memory's Throne'
Whereon you reign forever my dear love
My solace and my strength to face all strife
Then I shall lift my head and look above
Because you gave me courage to face life

(1940s)

Force of Nature

A grey set dawn – a cloudy scornful sky
Swift wind and waves combine to play
A sombre and gigantic symphony.

Music from Hell – a sulky day
When all the forces of nature combine
With fiendish laughter against man

Whose petty strife makes perpetual whine
And discord in the mighty plan
Of all the Universe.

(1940s)

The Arab Cloak

A man weaves for himself a beautiful cloak of dreams,
but it will not protect him,
though it wraps him from head to foot,
against the fury of the desert sandstorm. (Arab Proverb)

I wrapped myself in a cloak of dreams
Thinking I would be immune from pain
Dreams wear well by the light of Moonbeams
But are not proof against wind and rain
My dreams of you are all I have now
Of the sweetness we knew together
Sadly I place them away and vow
That I will cherish them forever

(1940s)

14

Yet Life Goes By

Still life goes by and uneventful seems
So dead am I who live within my dreams
That, though I seem to breathe and walk and speak
Still dead am I and all the world is bleak.

The stars that used to shine above at night
Seemingly now show half their former light
The sea has lost all might, the wind all force –
No sweetness in the once loved scent of gorse

(1940s)

New Chapters

I hold my baby 'neath my heart
And thought that she would be a part
Of my life in its even flow,
But now I find this is not so.
Of her life I'm an incident
Merely through birthly accident.
I think perhaps we all must make
This fond, possessive, blind mistake.

For in the early infant days –
We kindle love into a blaze
And hope it is a second chance
To live our lives again. Perchance
We dream that we shall re-create
Our old ideals and hoodwink fate
But cheat and strive thus though we may,
Our children live a different way.

For all my heartaches will not aid
My child to face life unafraid,
Because it is her right to learn
To love and hate – To fight and yearn
And nothing I can say or do
Will help her in her life come through
Untouched, by sorrow, trouble, trial
I guide her – for a little while.

But only whilst a baby she
Will cling to me – and only me.
So, while she's mine I'll have the joy
Of playing with my pretty Toy
And when we reach dividing ways
I'll stand with tear bemisted gaze
And hope this little ship will sail
A voyage fair to end her tale!

(c1944)

Winter Evenings

Dark red curtains to shut out the cold
A smokey fire with flames of gold
Deep comfy chairs and soft warm rugs
Old brass and copper pans and jugs
Reflect bright gleams from burning logs.

A purring cat and two old dogs
Soft music, cigarettes, and peace
Evenings and nights that never cease
To bring contentment and joy. – With you
I'll make this dream of mine come true

(1940s)

Lost Paradise

Autumnal leaves float drearily through air
Still dampened with the mist of early morn.
Of summer we have justly had full share
And now in lonely weariness, forlorn,
The heart hangs heavy as the wet dragged boughs.

The bitter wind chills in a dead embrace.
From deep despondency hope cannot rouse,
The trees show naked limbs devoid of grace
All round the chilly threat of winter shows
And soon the meadowlands will disappear
Beneath the heavy burden of the snows.
Black clouds will mourn the passing of the year
The world will see a dawning spring again,
Alas! we cannot Paradise regain.

(1944)

Heart's Loneliness

I laugh and talk and flirt a little, it is true,
My world is filled with men, but none of them are you.
My mind and body live and move, I breathe and eat
And wear a mask of gaiety that seems complete.

But when I see the moonbeams shine across the sea,
Or smell the blossom from the old Syringa tree
And hear the birds at dawning sing their lovely song
My soul fills with nostalgia and life seems wrong.
In all the lovely things I see each long day through

My heart pays homage to the memory of you.

(1944)

A Requiem

And it was written Centuries ago
When time was young and smiled on eager hearts
That - as the world grew old and seemed to know
A satiation whence all joy departs –
It should frown on such as you and I
Begrudging us our love, and calling fate
To make a mock – and joy to pass us by
Ah! my Beloved! we have met too late
Our love could make all history seem pale
Had Fortune smiled on us and let us meet
Before. But now it is of no avail
Our paths lie different ways, and we must greet
Each other in a light and trivial way
Because we, who belong, are not allowed
The Moon and Stars at night, or Sun by day
And our Secret is covered by the cloud
Of cynicism which the world will wear
Now that its blood runs slow and thin and cold.
This heavy cross is yours and mine to bear
Because we started life when time was old.

(1940s)

War Dreams

My daughter raised her grave blue eyes
Where raced across the summer skies
A crowd of fighter planes, a dream
Of beauty in a silvered scheme
Against the blue and white puffed sky.
I looked at her and wished that I
Could see them with the eyes of youth
And need not know the fearful truth,
The purpose there behind their flight,
And sighed at their symbolic might.

My daughter looked out from the shore,
And, as she spoke, I sighed once more.
'See! pretty ships' she cried with glee,
A convoy winding out to sea.
A grand heroic sight that brought
A memory of battles fought
In bygone years – with what result?
They did not save us this tumult!
All through the ages, then, must we
Endure these horrors ceaselessly?

'Look Tanks and Soldiers, Dear' said I
An armoured mass went pounding by
With slogans all chalked up in jest,
Going to battle – cheered and blessed.
With fevered minds the crowd there sang,
Deep in my heart I felt a pang
'The fools, do they believe their cries,
While the pick of England's future dies?
You dream your dreams, Oh! daughter mine
Reality is bitter wine.'   (1944)

A German Woman's Lament

I knew my country proud and fair in days gone by
I saw my husband go to war and heard him die
His choking wracks my memory – He was my pride
To spare him just one moments pain I would have died.
When he was gone I had to live, vain tho' it seemed
– I had a daughter and two sons. I strove and schemed,
I worked and went without that they may surely be
Part of a new and better world – too late for me.

But my beloved Fatherland fell into hands
Unworthy of the promise of these dear lands
I watched my sons grow tall and strong with bitter thought
Seeing Evil in the foul doctrine that they were taught
They took it with the eager grasp of growing youth,
When I demurred they would not heed – I spoke the truth.
The flags and bands do not aid them now – for one is dead
My eldest boy will never walk – nor earn his bread.

No home have I, for where I lived is desolate
I only wanted peaceful life – but swift cruel fate
Has robbed me of my simplest dreams, I am bereft
What holds the future for my girl – will she be left
To live amongst this chaos? Can I spare her pain?
Shall I, who love her, take her life? In vain
I try, but cannot see, a purpose in my sorrow
Oh God, of pity let me die – not face tomorrow.

(1940s)

The Promised Land

They called him to Field of Battle, to fight for his Native Land,
He left in a blaze of glory, with cheering crowds and a band.
They called it a War to end Wars, to establish a lasting peace
And they promised that when it was over, his worries all would cease.
He'd return to a Land fit for Heroes, full of kindness and beauty
and joy,
With a Job waiting ready for him, and a College built for his boy.
The Spectre of Suffering vanished, Security reigning instead -
A fitting and lasting Memorial to honour his Pals who were dead.

So he went through the horror of Flanders, with its slaughter, its filth
and its slime
Baptised in the Blood of Battle that changes men into swine
He saw his Comrades dying, in agonising pain,
Their stomachs slit to blazes – their sacrifice in vain.
He was sick at the sights around him, at times he was scarcely sane
For Satanic Scenes of Terror were imprinted on his brain.
But he looked into the Future, to the Land they'd promised him
And through all the heat of Battle, that Vision ne'er grew dim.

He returned to the Land of his Fathers, to celebrate and stay
They gave him a hearty welcome – and forgot him the very next day.
He found his old job was taken, there was nothing for him to do
At the Labour Exchange each morning, he stood with his pals in
a queue.
He was treated like an Outcast, he grew haggard and worn and old
For food for his starving children his soul he would have sold.
His Son grew anaemic and crooked, whose future he'd
planned with pride
He thought of his War Mates with envy – and wished that he
too had died.

Once again he is called to Battle, once again he's a Hero grand,
Once again the same old promise of a new and better land.
And Politicians wrangle on Post-War Planning Schemes
And Beveridge is scoffed at for his fantastic dreams.
What Fate awaits our Men-folk, when to ruins they return?
Shall they starve again while Profiteers their filthy lucre burn?
Shall we let them grow degenerate and force them to ways of crime?
My friend, if again this happens – the fault will be yours
and mine.

(1940s)

Voices from the Sea

Oh have you not heard them:
The voices from the sea?
Do they never call to you
The way they call to me?

I hear the calm and gentle tone
Of early morning calm
When not a ripple shows.

(1940s)

The Secret of the Sea

The Savour of Salt Breezes means more than Life to me,
For nigh on fifty years, my lads, I've sailed upon the sea.
I've seen strange sights and heard strange sounds beyond all human ken
And standing on the bridge at dawn, I've been a King of men
Yet less than Slave, for to the Wave I fain must bend the knee
For I can never fathom – the Secret of the Sea.

It sinks into the blood and bone, it penetrates the brain,
Drake and his gallants heard the Call upon the Spanish Main.
And every Seaman loud and rough who boasts and brawls in Port
Will feel its secret, silent strength and know he counts for nought.
It lures men to destruction, relentless, cold and grey
Yet gives new life to stricken souls who've fallen by the way.

Each wave murmurs a message that Sailors understand
The language of the sea is known in every distant land.
It links men in a Union no human hate can break
But from its faithful followers a heavy toll doth take.
Yet who can hear its call, my lads, and linger on the shore
We're old and feeble, but we've strength for just one voyage more.

We'll seek the Secret of the Sea – its triumph, joy and pain
We'll feel the wild winds lash against our bulwarks once again.
And if the Greatest Skipper should signal our small ship
We'll set sail for Eternity – the last and greatest trip.
For I reckon He who made the Sea will welcome you and me
And once aboard His Ship we'll know the Secret of the Sea.

(date unknown)

Depression

Christmas – the time when lonely souls
Withdraw still further in their shells
Away from sentimental deeds
And from glad joyful pealing bells.

In the surging sea and the swiftness of the gale
Dread sorrows, ghostly voices, mingle and bewail
Lost souls seeking peace, with restless frightful weeping
Toads with bloated bodies wrapped in peace – sleeping.

(1940s)

After the Nightmare

A dreamer wakens striving to release
From greeny depths, a mind all hung with weeds
Slowly and softly a returning ease
Pervades the dreamer's senses and the beads
Upon the curtains rattle in the breeze
The sun is warm upon the glass – he reads.

(1940s)

Boy? Man!

A mother thinks of days gone by
A little boy who would not cry
But blinked back tears lest she should see
A weakness – not for such as he
Who prowls the quarterdeck and cries
'Come! Varlets, here is Merchandise,
Fine silks and tea from old Cathay
My lusty lads, come – we'll away
And take our precious treasure to
A Coral Isle in seas of blue!'

That mother hopes for days to be
When her son comes home from the sea
He'll be her little boy no more,
For he had sailed from shore to shore
Of all the Seven Seas and now
A man is he, with broad calm brow,
Set jaw and steady eyes of blue
Have all his boyhood dreams come true?
Mother – you should be proud and say
My son? He is a man today!

(1940s)

Intellectual Heights

Climb you down that lonely hill
At the bottom runs a rill
To quench the thirst and cool the feet
The place where you and I can meet
Climb you down that lonely hill.

Climb you down that lonely hill
Come you when the air is still
I cannot give you heady heights
Just simple, human, sweet delights
Climb you down that lonely hill.

(1940s)

To My Mother

(In memory of Olga Dorothea Porter,
died 25th November 1946, aged 50)

There seemed to be something huge and important to say;
But somehow, then, we would never think of the words.
Anyway, they would keep, so it did not matter,
And there would be time and time enough to remember;
So we laughed as the years flew over our heads like birds.

And then, one day, we remembered them; ran all the way,
Breathless, came running, and beat and called at your door –
At the door of a house whose silence and emptiness mocked us;
For you had slipped out the back way, quite quietly, leaving
'I love you, and thank you,' unneeded, unsaid, ever more.

Peace

Incensed hush at morning Mass
Sunrise gleams through stained glass
Solemn words, sonorous tone
Peaceful sense of being alone
Yesterdays or tomorrows
Happiness against sorrows
Organ softly murmurs. Peace.
Must this wonder ever cease.

(1940s)

Poems written
after 1946

After the War:
Betty and Ken Jump at Bognor,
1950

Was and Is

Time was –
When birds would sing
And bells would ring
And everything

Time is –
When no birds sing
And no bells ring –
and nothing.

(May 1975)

The Lost Child

In memory of Louise

When the long night greys into dawn
And I, sleepless lie
Soft shadows on the dew-wet lawn,
Gone the night wind's sigh.

I think of her, my baby, lost –
See with tear-dry eye
Her infant face, with hair curl-tossed,
Hear her gentle cry.

Soft peace has come into my breast –
Even with a sigh.
I held her once, in arms warm-pressed,
Loved – in days gone by.

Lament For A Dead Child

Borne upon the still night air
There came a baby's cry
And she wakened to despair
To know nobody was there –
For her child had to die.

Still the sound of sobbing came
Sadly in her sorrow
Whispering, soft, her baby's name,
Clutching at her picture frame
Came the grey tomorrow.

'Bleak the day, bereft am I,
Long the empty years will seem.
When I hear my baby cry
My heart despairs while tears are dry
Remembering my dream.'

(1980)

Shades and Echoes

Who are those children
Playing in the shadows?
Two small girls and a little boy,
Gentle shades of love
From so long ago –
Children, my children where are you now?

Where are those children
Who played in the shadows?
My two small daughters and my son. Grown and flown
away,
Gone – so long ago,
Days passed, years passed, left me their echoes.

Tell me ghost children
Who met in the shadows,
Golden girls and a nut brown boy
Will you think of me
When, on sun bright days
Your children play?

(1972)

The Lost Love

My love was mine and I was His
And now my love has gone
For him love's transient brief bliss
Now run it's course and done.
But ah! my heart is always his
And Oh! my days are long
And all my mind can hear is this
Nostalgic sweet sad song.

He was not mine but I am his
For all my life shall last,
My lips still feeling his last kiss,
My future is my past.

(1973)

Pussy Willow

Oh, much loved golden cat we miss
Your purry ways, your sleepy bliss.
All curiosity and fun,
Your wilful presence now is gone
And when the Hunter's moon appears
You nevermore will twitch your ears
And creep, flat bellied, on the ground
Or leap with one big steel sprung bound
Relentlessly upon your prey,
Nor stretch in summer sun all day.
Dear Golden Cat we see you still
Behind the springtime daffodil
And in the dusk of night time sky
We feel your shadow slipping by.

(1976)

Joe the Dog

I had a dog
Whose name was Joe
And my young self
Did love him so.

And Joe, my Joe
Would run and play
Where e'er we'd go
Each lovely day.

But I grew tall
And Joe grew old
And soon was all
His story told.

When sweet winds blow
Or burns Yule Log
I think of how
I loved my dog.

And though he's gone
Now I am old
His love has shone
To warm my cold.

Ah! Joe are you
Awaiting me
When I come
To Eternity?

(1973)

The Wedding

Wedding morn,
Up since dawn,
And everything goes well.

Bride all dressed,
And the rest
As if by magic spell

Organ plays
Hymns of praise
And the service starts.

Vows exchanged
Veil arranged,
Joy in our happy hearts.

Pictured all,
Smile, stand tall
Love, kisses, speeches done.

Change of gear,
Mrs here,
A hug before you're gone.

Goodbye Love,
May life prove
to hold great happiness.

We stand here,
Just one tear,
Goodbye to both – God Bless.

(1976)

When I was Young and Sad

Time was when I was young and sad
And life seemed worthless at the start
And love and hate were good and bad
But nothing really touched my heart.

It seemed as though I stood outside
And none of it was meant for me.
What kept me going was my pride
The emptiness of being free.

There should be something more,
I thought. Or why the lovely melodies?
Could nature's lessons be self taught
With knowledge whispered on the breeze.

Time is and I am older, glad
To know that life has been worthwhile,
With all the whole world to be had
Within the love shown in your smile.

(1976)

What is Poetry?

Life cried out 'What is poetry?'
And my young self replied 'I know not'.
The seeking permeated youth
With never-ending search for truth.
But truth is not poetry
And life ticked on
'til youth had gone.

Love called out 'What is poetry?'
My deluded self said 'I know now'
But disillusionment began
Poetry is not one man
And love is not poetry.
The days flicked on
But love had gone.

Age said 'What is poetry?'
And maturity replied 'I know less'
But acceptance helps perception
With more than one conception
Perhaps Life is poetry
In every phase
Of blame and praise?

(1977)

A Practical Man

Oh! send to me a practical man
With whom my life to share.
Who better than a practical man
Of me to take good care.

An Adonis may be thrilling
Or a poet may be willing
To let me be his slave.
A tycoon could be dynamic,
A James Bond cause me panic
'Cos I'm not very brave!

But send to me a practical man
With whom my life to share,
A warm and loving handyman
This is my earnest prayer!

(1977)

The Re-arranged

Last night I dreamed I walked the shore again
As, long ago I walked upon the shore;
In sun and shade, in gentle summer rain,
In winter watched the storm tossed waters roar.

In youth, long lost to me, the seasons passed
When all my secrets and my fears I took
And walked away the many burdens, first and last,
Until my nursery rhyme became a book.

So, I, away from my beloved shore,
Have passed my years and changing, never changed
The instinct that the sea forever more
Has power to re-arrange the re-arranged.

(1978)

Time's Twist

I have returned and here will stay
Among scenes of my youth.
The exiled years bore happy days
Best of my life, in truth.

But here I sang my growing song
Among my friends and peers;
And, on return they are all gone
And I, alone, walk here

There is a price of growing old
Which, paid by loved ones missed!
And all the tales of youth are told
But time has made a twist.

My tale of age is new, it's true,
But oh! the gaps it leaves
With each remembered shadow who
Passed on – and so – one grieves.

Years Passed

The Years have passed my Valentine
Since I was yours and you were mine.
And in the years all things have been
Joy, sorrow, and in between
The certainty that you were there
To dry my tears, end my despair

To share the good times and the bad
Such lovely memories we've had.
All I ever wanted was you
I've had, and loved, your love so true
My thanks, with all my heart, are here
In these few words, my dearest dear.

The Lake

Around the lake the bracken grows
Faded and gone is Summer's rose
And all the browns and golds portray
With falling leaves, our own decay.

When Spring is smiling on the lake
All carelessly of life partake,
Tomorrow follows all tomorrows,
Youth ignores life's promised sorrows.

But now the hidden shiver seeks
To surface in these golden weeks,
With heightened senses to behold
The poignant fate – of growing old

(1980)

The Last Spring

In bloom I saw the daffodils
This sad, this last, this lovely Spring,
And saw the mauve and distant hills,
And heard the mating birds who sing.

To know that nevermore will I
See gentle dusk or stars that gleam,
Or sunset or bright summer sky –
Here ends this life, this love, this dream.

(1983)

My Son

My son, my little son, when you were born
At noon upon a summer day,
Sweet Jasmine scent hung heavy all the morn
Around the bed on which I lay.

Then when they placed you safely in my arm
And I beheld your small dark head,
There resting in the welcome post-birth calm
I watched your tiny fingers spread.

Now the long waiting months are left behind
Of the wondering who you'd be,
Through time the umbilical cord will bind,
In years ahead, both you and me.

(1984)

The Real World

Reality is far from dreams
As sun is from the moon
But dreams are opiate it seems
For disillusioned June.

With moon synonymous with love
And June with sweet romance,
Then youth with hopes of skies above
Is apt to take a chance.

With nature the deceiver ever
We're led by nose and tail
To spurn old June and moon forever
And lift the real world's veil.

By then, yes then, we really see
The beauty that is hidden
In lessons life gives us for free
Comes life and love unbidden.

(1985)

Ode to Pain

Pain! You clench your iron hand upon my being
And twist, and my poor mortal soul rebels,
For the torment colours and invades my seeing
And drains the strength, from stones in secret wells.

My not-so-iron will submits and there my pride
Lies, down in the dust, in broken tatters.
At least allow me the resolve to put aside
My pain, in public, when most it matters.

(1984)

My Blessing

May your feet leave happy footprints
Upon the sands of time.

May all the words you ever say
Make sense in one great rhyme.

May all the kindness and the love
Live ever in your heart.

May all the beauty that you see
To those you love impart.

To All my Loves

Do not put flowers on my grave –
or give a grave to me
Just scatter me upon the heights,
Or valleys – or the sea.

Just think of me, once in a while
Upon a sunny day,
Or when you see a baby smile
Or on a wedding day.

(March 1991)